RUN AWAY TO THE YARD

Run Away to the Yard

poems by

Lisa C. Krueger

Red Hen Press | *Pasadena, CA*

Book layout by Stephanie Lopez

Library of Congress Cataloging-in-Publication Data
Names: Krueger, Lisa C., author.
Title: Run away to the yard / poems by Lisa C. Krueger.
Description: First edition. | Pasadena, CA : Red Hen Press, [2017]
Identifiers: LCCN 2016048421 | ISBN 9781597090261 (pbk. : alk. paper) |
    ISBN 9781597090285 (casebound)
Classification: LCC PS3611.R84 A6 2017 | DDC 811/.6—dc23
LC record available at https://lccn.loc.gov/2016048421

The National Endowment for the Arts, the Los Angeles County Arts Commission, the Dwight Stuart Youth Foundation, the Max Factor Family Foundation, the Pasadena Tournament of Roses Foundation, the Pasadena Arts & Culture Commission and the City of Pasadena Cultural Affairs Division, the City of Los Angeles Department of Cultural Affairs, the Audrey & Sydney Irmas Charitable Foundation, Sony Pictures Entertainment, Amazon Literary Partnership, and the Sherwood Foundation partially support Red Hen Press.

First Edition
Published by Red Hen Press
www.redhen.org

ACKNOWLEDGMENTS

Acknowledgments are made to the editors of the following publications in which some of these poems or variations of these poems appeared or will appear:

Barrow Street: "Casilda at the Norton Simon"; *Clark Street Review*: "Case Notes in Red"; *December*: "Camphor"; *Mid-American Review*: "Violet on a Plane"; *Miramar*: "Reverent"; *Nimrod*: "Parallax at Nine a.m." and "The Latin of It"; *Oberon*: "Personal Taste"; *Ploughshares*: "Outside the Rialto"; *Poet Lore*: "Breathing Room"; and *The Tishman Review*: "Intimacy."

"Parallax at Nine a.m." and "The Latin of It" received finalist recognition for the Pablo Neruda Poetry Prize.

My deepest gratitude to Kate Gale, Mark Cull, Mark Wunderlich, and Jim Moore; and to my beloved family and friends.

For Family

CONTENTS

I

II

III

RUN AWAY TO THE YARD

*This book is a work
of the imagination.*

I have walked through many lives,
some of them my own,
and I am not who I was,
though some principle of being
abides, from which I struggle
not to stray.

—Stanley Kunitz

PASSINGS

The summer was just starting yet
like a fast ride it was over.
The man and the woman arrived at the end;

everywhere they sensed
the night blooms and crickets.
They yearned for the clean, ironed

sheets of blue sky
that folded into the past.
The man and the woman stood in the yard

by the hammock she loved.
A dry breeze rocked
the emptiness.

They wished they could lie down,
balance their bodies like the old days.
The sun sank, they smelled jasmine,

the breeze crested in waves.
Memory washed across them,
they swayed, amazed.

VIOLET ON A PLANE

The girl across the aisle closes then opens her
hands the way flowers surrender to light, a slow
devotion. She watches her fingers uncurl to
stillness. *Sit down, Violet,* mother says to child.
Please sit down. Sky becomes violet. Women
watch reflections of themselves fly into darkness.
Mother folds her arms around child, their hands
touch palm to palm as though making a pact.
How much is one person allowed? A woman
who longs to lose herself forgets the scent of
violets. She believes it was sweet.

OUTSIDE THE RIALTO

She is crushing on a younger guy after many conversations about things like the brain's musical notations or quinoa recipes. His round face, wire rims almost ubiquitous, almost like every young man at work. She tells her husband about the crush, he thinks it's probably good for her. When she talks to her crush she forgets to feel old. After a few weeks she thinks maybe she loves him, not in an older-woman-stalking kind of way, but in a spiritual sense. Part of her just wants to be him, or wants him to be part of her. It feels harmless, the way they talk, laugh. When her crush dies unexpectedly, she plunges into a strange mourning. She doesn't cry, doesn't dream of him but begins to walk with a limp. Nothing hurts, her body just wants to limp, as though nursing a sprain. Her husband comes with her to the service. Standing-room only, a cacophony of hipsters, young families, matrons. Friend after friend goes forward to talk about his gardening groups, his Sunday afternoon mai tais, the concerts. Madonna, how the man loved Madonna. His mother cries, asking everyone to cherish his memory, the dad stands next to her, silent. Divorced yet still they hug. Toward the end when the theater gets dusky and people shift around, shredding damp tissues, she feels overcome with a need to talk, to declare how beautiful he was to her, how she is learning to walk again. A woman near her speaks out, saying almost exactly what she wanted to say, using words she would have chosen. Outside the Rialto afternoon light crystallizes in prisms against the theater's deco façade. Her crush's partner is smoking, leaning against the pillars. He comments to everyone who passes, *This is my last one, I swear.*

INTEGUMENTARY

Of course the children grow up

and leave. She learns

to avoid babies—just touching them

sparks cataclysms, history's

igneous pinprick. She wants

the science of skin,

its sea of cells constricting

against the intimate sting.

Yet the newborn next door!

When she cradles him

her hands have no buffer,

she feels the baby's imprint.

She used to mother

without fear, release everything

just to quiet them.

Here, she would say.

Here. Take this. This.

Take me. Take anything.

SANTA MONICA BIRTH

Someone decapitated all Birds of Paradise
along Ocean Avenue; strollers and shoes

trample the discarded beaks. She keeps walking.
At noon a hallway speaker booms

Code Blue Code Blue one minute
before her grandson is born.

In the evening, a nurse hands him
to her: clean, swaddled, murmuring:

the fullness of his being spears her.
Why didn't I pick them up? she wonders,

arms tightening around the infant,
whispers *I still carry you!* to her son

when he comes to take his child.

MOTEL FOR THE LEAVE OF ABSENCE

Early morning in a dingy lobby, the sound of highway trucks coming through closed windows. She pushes the dispenser buttons, no coffee comes out. *Strange*, she says, noticing the teenager next to her. He is rocking back and forth with an empty cup. Tall, slightly beefy in a misbuttoned shirt, *Like one of my sons*, she thinks, *that morning face*, semi-shaved, dispassionately present. The boy speaks, *They touched my mama*, punches at the machine, *Took her away*, rocking, rocking. She looks at him directly. *Go sit down, Ryan, go sit*, a man says. Tall and thin, plaid shirt buttoned correctly, face fallen with something so familiar her own face burns: *Come, Son*. The boy is singing: *So long, farewell, auf Wiedersehen adieu*, the man guiding him to a table. *Adieu, adieu*, looking at her as though he knows whom she has left. *Sshh, hush now*, the cowboy says, reading the paper, holding his hand.

EVE

She sits on the grass with her magazine,
gardenia slices the air. At senior prom, the boy
pinned a corsage to her dress, slipped his finger

down her breast. Flowers and a feeling
of drowning. *This is who I am,*
letting him touch her more, waiting for the feeling

to end. It lasted years. She called it youth.
The children are whirling, laughing,
willing themselves to fall again and again.

The cover of *Country Living* is all celebrity—
a star in miniskirt with boots, her famous man
strumming his guitar, *Kick Back in Style.*

She takes off her shoes. The snake writhes
near her foot. *You again,* she says, leaning close
to study his skin's diamond design.

SWIM ALONE

He clings to her while other boys
play Marco Polo. A year of lessons,
this is what she gets?

She wants to lie in the sun.
Enough, she says, loosens her arms,
releases him. The boy winces at light

bouncing off water. He grasps at her,
where he thinks she is, but feels blind.
He decides to drown for his mother.

Just this morning he breathed only when
she breathed, laughed when she laughed.
Before he goes under he hears one boy

catch another: *My eyes were closed!*
His cries, underwater, make bubbles
that rise like loose balloons.

He watches his mother's legs
move away. Out of breath, he swims
toward empty blue.

PRACTICE

Devotion is for the children:
she will do anything for them.
Music must live in crevices of her life,

music must wait. She practices silent hours
in sleepless nights, rehearses a genius
she vows to recall. Skin pressing hard

against string. Half-noted hesitance, its lyric
history of diminution, gives way to a larger sound.
Fingers feel the cadence of possibility.

This instrument is a miracle, she tells herself,
watching the violin, watching her body
as though from above. Every morning

she listens to her youngest hum,
knowing his child voice won't last.
She wants to memorize everything.

All her life, searching for position—
how to hold this precious thing—
afraid of her wayward touch.

PROVIDER

A pink plastic cup perches on the bald spot of the daddy's head. He squats by the stroller to distract his daughter—smiles, kisses the air. Every time he returns from a trip he wonders if she remembers him. *Do babies worry?* he thinks, the cup beginning to slide, a lopsided clown's hat. She still cries. He reaches for the bottle his wife expressed, remembering she didn't want to give it to him: *Don't go too far.* He studies the community's gated edge, his daughter fusses at the fake nipple. *You only want your mother,* he says, turning them back. He begins to tell her about trips, what he eats, what he watches on the hotel TVs, astonished at mourning.

ECHO AT THE FESTIVAL OF LIGHT

He had not expected so many women, some dressed in those knit suits his wife used to wear, some in jeans so tight he wonders how they walk. Milling around glass cases lit like a stage, klieg lights too bright. *Jewelry Sale*, says the sign, what a day to choose. *Mix and Match*, something about a collection of charms. He doesn't understand. Everywhere women's voices—*This is so cute!* Everywhere women buying bits of gold. He stands by the diamond case, feels translucent. A clerk with large hair comes at him, looks angry when he says he has a repair. *What what*, she says. He shows her the ring. *Resizing*, she says. *Put it on.* The ring's insignia burns against his papery hand. *This is so big it's impossible*, she says, studying him as though he stole it. *It was my son's*, he whispers, hearing the words reverberate. *Well, sorry. Let me see*, she says, walking away with the ring.

SANTA ANITA MALL

Hello Kitty on suitcases, toasters, bejeweled cellphones; girls in bathing suits hawking Dead Sea scrub; islands of cinnamon-sugar pretzels, enchilada-flavored popcorn, attach-your-own-photo dolls. A clerk points the plastic gun at a baby's lobe and shoots, mother and grandmother laughing, gripping the baby's head. Spectators yawn from the other side of glass. Her own granddaughter holds a stud chart, chooses green *like nature*. Crying baby reflections swirl with racks of cupcake earrings. The next girl in line whispers, *Try other piercings. The pain is fun.*

THE LATIN OF IT

Oleander's fuchsia petals would scatter-shot
center divides of the 5, the 110;
her LA, her *urbs angelicorum*.

When she was young, every street
had oleander, every kid reached
for the dangerous bloom.

Don't touch, her mother had said.
Don't touch, she told her children.
A neighbor lost the custody battle

then steeped leaves for tea; she didn't
completely die. An oleander memory,
a *Nerium memoria*.

Oleander perished from bacterium
Xylella fastidiosa. On her freeways,
concrete barriers replace their skeletons.

She once held the scent
of her babies' skin,
the *flore delicatus* of caress—

MAP OF RETURN

Her son bore the weight
of another man's mother,
three to each side
of the casket.
His college roommate,
the grieving son,
walked behind him.
She felt so light,
he tells his mother,
but carrying her
became hard.
She still called him
on Sundays, he says,
like you.
She used to wish away
her children's pain.
Sorrow, finding its place,
brings her close to him;
for the afternoon
distance doesn't exist.

TRANSIENT

Her father said God was the sea.
When they scattered his ashes, waves
carried them back—flecks of mica,

grains of bone veiled the shore.
She told her children God was everything,
they could pray to the sunset.

Can I pray to this cracker?
one of them asked: sitting
at breakfast, smiling at one another

like the early days.
Her father was a Kansas boy.
His grandchildren never knew him.

Once they found seashells
in a Midwest cornfield.
Are these miracles? one asked.

They were alone, surrounded
by land and sky, on their knees
gathering cowries and sand dollars.

Over time, the discoveries dissolved
into backpacks and duffels,
bedside tables and memory jars.

II

CALL ME JOEL

The mariachis and donkey arrive. Their
sombreros have gold tassels, the donkey
wears a gold serape. Guests show up
already drunk. Everyone is "Mr." and
"Mrs." One man says, *Call me Joel. You
better call me Joel.* If she keeps moving,
everything seems the same. She walks
to her brother at the bar, the bartender
offers her a margarita. After sunset the
people laugh extra loud, their faces jump
in tiki torchlight. For a while she thinks
she understands why her father drinks—
the whole world loosens. Joel asks her if
she wants to dance, she says, *No thank you
Mr. Barrett.* Men in suits push each other
into the pool, there is broken glass by the
edge. She wonders if anyone is happy. The
donkey circles the yard, swaying under
women in cocktail dresses that ride up
their thighs.

TOUGH NEWS

Girl at the Bar scrolling her phone
with sensuous thumb strokes kicks
the woman's purse absentmindedly,
rhythmically. The woman leans in with
her friend, nursing drinks, discussing
the tough news. No energy to pull her
bag away. She endures a regular thump
against her calf until something Girl
at the Bar reads seems to bring her up
short. Then Girl laughs and laughs as
though her laughter will never stop.

THE LAX BODY
WAS A RIVER

She gets up, pretends
it is morning. She can't
remember the way she
used to sleep, wonders
if fear ever leaves once
it makes a home. Only
last year she thought
dreams were a gift.
Visualize a body of
water: nightmares flow
away. She swims in a sea
of desire.

DUE TO AN EMERGENCY

The surgeon herself comes in to
explain that due to an emergency,
there is a delay. When they are alone
again, he joins her on the gurney.
They talk about noise of the past,
how the children had filled space with
commotion so intense they thought
they needed respite, any kind of
vacation for some quiet. They never
did get away, never really wanted to.

WHEN SHE CAN'T BREATHE

Monarchs and hollow-
boned treeswifts

fly crooked
in the drought,

their fine gristle
of color razors

her eyes. *Pain is not
an epiphany, ok?*

she says aloud,
studying the thought

that she did this
to herself.

From her bed
she imagines flying,

imagines forgiveness
as ruptured sky.

GRAY HERON, SANTA ANA WINDS

Drought-parched grass
nicks skin when she lies down,

unbuttons her shirt, scars tender:
once she was whole.

A heron with broken wings
crawls across her yard, bulky,

misplaced, a dinosaur bird.
For one afternoon, she believes

any god will do.
Heal me, she beseeches.

In baldness. Bowing
to feathered vestment.

VAST ROOM

Next to the water cooler and
bowl of pink-ribbon candy stands
a television, Ozymandias of
the infusion center. Colossal,
commanding—at first, everyone
watches it. She used to gaze at its
regular conversion from bright-
striped aquarium fish to weeping
rainforests, followed by tropical
islands where waves slope toward
unblemished sand. Now she
watches the other women. Pale
faces and wigs puff out like they
are underwater. Some study the
screen. Some study her.

INFUSED

She calls out to sea
and sea listens.
Walks toward breakers
without fear, water
against her hips,
pulling her down.
Sometimes, lost
in surf's white light,
she thinks *I will stay
underwater.*
Sometimes she can't
remember earth.

ANOINTED

She thinks about a white light the healer said could bathe her body, shield it from harm. Lying alone, listening to a distant train and a sound of leaves falling. Lake of white light; ghost of white light: she begins to pray for the drought in everyone's heart. She remembers the white of her son when he knelt at the altar. She used to tell her children that God was everywhere. After the anointment, her son's white robe was stained with oil. He made the sign of the cross. The cathedral was filled with oil-stained supplicants, people everywhere in white.

CASILDA AT THE NORTON SIMON

Saint Casilda was very ill.
Yet smiled through anguish.
Yet transformed bread to roses.

The woman studies Casilda's
pallid portrait, feels pain again,
not fire but dull night. *Casilda*:

She changes her name.
Walks past masterpieces (lemon,
cup, platter of game)

to the post-constructed world.
Stops at a café. Nearby,
bankers argue takeovers;

a woman shares soup
with a coifed dog.
Casilda builds a composition:

bread, bouquet, ordinary saint. No
healing waters. No feast of fallen fruit,
pheasant with a broken neck.

ENTRANCE

When the woman meditates, she falls asleep.
When she sleeps, she thinks.

Waking in the dark, dreaming
she has missed another day:

at the doctor's office a kid signs in
long after her, talks to everyone

about his aching back
from feeding the homeless.

Aww, says the receptionist,
Come on in.

The woman scrolls her cell with indignation,
scrunches over to decipher

miniscule messages. Suffering
has made everything small.

Later, strong enough to walk
down her street, she watches

ginkgos change, shedding gold
like lovers dispensing with clothes

in a rush, even though
it is autumn, and cold.

RUN AWAY TO THE YARD

He plays his harmonica

watching her

through the window

she could suffocate

on indoor solace,

needs respiration

of dirt and bark

willow leaves fall

in syncopated staccato

his melody from memory

is muffled

the tone resonates

in her throat

like the river they

crossed on foot

submerging themselves

in song

CONTAINED

My home. My things, she thinks, *the sand dollars, the dried flowers,* noticing a stack of photos and cards on the floor. She will place them in a jar or basket or colorful box. *You collect too much,* says one of her children. He stands in front of the bed, looks at her in amazement: *What are we going to do with all this stuff?*

CLEAN SCANS

That night she dreams about a star in an unfamiliar constellation, a star that offers light in verses, like a song. She wishes she could find a name. When she wakes she can barely remember the whole incident. Yet all morning she repeats to herself, quietly, *I am*.

PARALLAX AT NINE A.M.

Can't locate herself. Children are calling again, one to complain about work, one to ask for money. Everything feels immediate and necessary. Unloading the dishwasher, step-by-step. Late summer presses at her, smell of peaches on the counter, gardenias in a vase. Cut grass and early smog, its bleached, burned tingle. Since when is the body slow? Dishes can take forever. *Hurry up*, her mind commands. Loneliness has no season. Birthing, breast-feeding, solace-keeping only change the weather. She wonders where all the dishes went, turning this way and that. *I am sorry, I am sorry*, she says to the receiver.

BAD GIRL

When she was ten her father left her
at a Denny's—*You'll get back.*

She walked the other way for miles
before a car pulled over, a man shouted

You are lost, opened his door to her.
Beyond him was darkness.

No lights, no signs, no people
telling her what to do:

she kept walking. Upright, strident,
terrified by her act.

Terrified she was bad
for saving herself.

They are very young: when they talk they hold hands, their lives beginning to join like trees rooted in one spot of earth, entwined until the separation of branch. Then they are not young yet still they sit hand in hand at the fairs and flea markets. They buy their own shop, a home of artifacts, crosses, angels. They love old things, love to touch them. Sometimes he uses a small knife to carve animals from wood, sometimes she weaves. Everything around them is for sale. Bestsellers are the hands of Jesus. No one buys the crucifix Jesus, so they pry him off. Sometimes the hands come loose. They feel happy. They are bothered for a while by computers, don't understand them, don't grasp the ether of images, they like the real thing. When business dries up they move into a rental room without a fireplace. Their wingback chairs, bookshelves, artifacts rent with them. The room feels cluttered, they discuss trying the internet for sales or maybe just giving everything away. Talking, holding onto each other.

The wife states that *The Boy* starts small fires and pisses in other children's backpacks. Looking at her husband, then looking away, she says these problems are only *Red Flags*, the *Biggest Red* is no sex in the home. The husband slouches. The wife is sick of seeing his *Red Ferrari* parked all over town, people are talking. He sits up to say that everyone knows about the affair with her boss. Her face reddens, a deep flush, almost a look of excitement. She begins to pace. He lies down on the couch. She raises her voice. He closes his eyes. The therapist suggests *reflective listening*. The wife says that they take turns sleeping with *The Boy* because he has nightmares. The husband, still supine, remarks that maybe she should wear something besides a negligee on those nights. The therapist comments that this is not effective communication. The wife stands over the husband and shouts that it is all his fault, he spends so much time trying to *get out of the Red* that they have no life. She is glistening with sweat. He continues to lie on the couch, body slack but for the erection.

BREATHING ROOM

When the guys leave for another round,
they start to catch up on gossip
until her friend leans in close, blouse
just above the salsa. Her friend whispers

I don't want it anymore—nothing's left,
gesturing at the bar. *What? What?*
she replies, picturing her friend's husband
reaching in the dark for emptiness.

I rented a room, her friend says,
He doesn't know.
I just need to breathe.
The men return, loom above them

while one finishes a story:
all she can see is pants. She wants
to ask her friend what a room costs
and does it work better with no stuff,

just the bareness she dreams about,
but her friend's husband
bends down with the wine,
his bald spot right next to her.

Her friend touches him on the back
of his neck—that caress
after love when everything
that can happen has happened.

INTIMACY

Now they say
Do not cover a baby!
when a baby sleeps.
Let an infant lie
without a blanket
or stuffed animal
or the near warmth
of another. Research
links closeness
with sudden death.
The woman stands
still, holds one who,
newly emerged,
burrows his head
into her chest, stops
crying, falls asleep.
She lays him in a bare
crib, watches his limbs
fall open to emptiness.
She, too, could sleep
in bareness, breathe
as she needs.
She, too, could use
absence to survive.

PERSONAL TASTE

They mix rituals: each dips a wafer in wine, a finger in honey. He stamps on a glass. She licks his finger. Outside the church, friends throw lavender; small purple pellets stick to hair. They climb into a Bentley with penis graffiti. At the reception the best man cries, ignores personal space. Bridesmaids yank strapless dresses that sneak down their breasts. Bar glasses shiver from band amplification. The bride's mother slow-dances with another woman, ignores the dad. At outer tables a guest with two left feet takes a fork to untouched cake. Everyone has known for years she can't dance. She moves with grace from plate to plate, aware that cake gets sweeter as it sits.

DUE DATE

Pastel-chested finches carry
twigs and string, cram
tiny nests into crevices
of the porch like warriors.

A kind of bird fury
is underway, as though
no one could stop them.
Whoever saw love as kind?

At the hospital, every infant
arrives like a miracle
in thin disguise. New mothers,
tied loosely in the back,

act royal yet perplexed
at those who jump up
and down in their old
people suits as though

the world came to an end
then started all over.

CAMPHOR

Listening for sounds

that the baby is awake

she hears insouciant wind

through a camphor tree.

In these canyons

a pacific light

bathes the homes: LA

hills create harbors.

People are never who

she wants them to be

yet as long as it takes

here she is

waiting.

AFTER WORDS

Once when she thought it could be over
the day's fever began to release from them

leaving a reverie of cool she didn't recognize.
They sat on the patio watching their garden,

how plants stiffened by heat
were relaxing into the dusk.

I am really afraid, she said, *Do you hear*
that I am afraid? and he said

Don't be negative, grasping her hand.
From across the yard a mother hawk

and baby flew down toward them
then soared up and away. Wild parrots

came next, then willow finches.
His head was turned,

she could feel him crying.
Shadows diminished. Starlings sang.

UNATTACHED

Awake in the night pretending to sleep through what they thought they could not bear. No respiration of a dream's feather. Each of them still, as though movement might prevent sleep's oblivion. Then one asks, *Remember the blueberries in Vermont?* A disembodied voice. They reminisce about berry picking, how every field harbored a harvest once they looked. How some fruit resisted so much they wanted to give up; it could stay there and rot. Then the bushes where everything fell into their hands. Reaching for a feast they didn't earn, no one can predict.

PREDATOR

She stood at the edge of the yard,
watched the coyote rub its back
against the redwood.

Her dogs barked from the kitchen
to chase the wildness
they waited for, LA suburbia

yielding at dusk to possums,
skunks, arroyo jackals. She smelled
native plants' night scent.

Go away, she cried to the bone-sack
of mange. Sun had settled in his eyes.
She couldn't make him leave.

She couldn't make anything leave—
the illness, the people
who made her want to live.

Go away, she called again,
the animal's gaze
burning through her.

FOREVER

No one knows whether
this is our only life
even when things like
autumn happen:
two people who
are crazy about foliage
drive for hours
to wonder at colors
and the juice of apples
they stop to pick
at orchards that charge
too much per pound
thinking they could do this
forever yet they are hungry
and head home for
cheese sandwiches
they eat while standing
and watching the other,
what they always do.

SUNDAY AFTERNOONS

The man falls asleep against her,
his head angled as when he read

to their children, pages of a book
wide open so everyone could see.

The children would giggle, their faces
lifting with desire. They wanted

to sit on his lap forever. The man
begins to laugh, as people do

in sleep, stirring, reaching for his wife.
She gazes ahead, listening,

a sound that is no sound
making its way across the lawn.

DONATING THE CAKE DOME

She couldn't stop—she did it
almost every afternoon while

they napped or later sat
upstairs with homework.

She listened to the scrape
of desk chairs on the ceiling

while she measured and blended,
hummed from oven

to sink, redolence rising
in a sweet promise she thought

was required, didn't know
how to live without,

all her life afraid
to be empty-handed.

OTHERS IN TOPANGA

Children leap stone to stone in the dry creek.
Her grandson runs to join them, his top-siders
skid against the steep paths parched slick.

She almost wishes he would slip just
to feel that elation of risk. She misses
the hippies who lived in these hollows.

She used to study the way they cooked,
slept, made love. If she waved,
they waved back.

Every night, she dreams of the boy
in shifted shapes—one who leaps
over boulders as Frog

or reconfigures light as Cloud. Always
beyond reach. If she could still climb,
she would show him the canyon's

hidden caves. Children below gather
around a leaf—or a smartphone. No one
looks up. Shadows scurry away.

NO QUIET

This morning she jogs past a man
who carries an empty KFC bucket
and a white balloon. He stumbles
down Kalakaua Avenue: *And*

the Northern girls, with the way
they kiss . . . He looks like her
high school boyfriend but
both of their bodies are battered.

She wants to tell him everything
will be OK even though she's no longer
sure. Some friends who live by the sea
take it for granted, don't even notice

the waves, the color of Pacific skin
at dawn. Lately she rises in the dark
just to study the glisten, just to watch
the water face another day.

WRITTEN

Eventually, every sound was a wave.
Perhaps, she heard herself say, *his words
arrived too late. He is no longer
a boy, I no longer a young mother.*

They were late as two strangers
standing at a bus stop, one peering
toward his destination, the other
reading and re-reading her past.

Don't ever write about me again.
Words, waves, crested, crashed.
Between them was the afternoon
she taught him to use a pencil,

screw what the teacher had said,
*Just grasp it in your fist and make
your mark, messy or dark,* she had said,
it doesn't matter, it's yours.

REVERENT

Her grandsons ran naked
through sprinklers,

hopped in her fountain
to swashbuckle.

Stepped out in boldness,
made footprints on brick.

Then handprints.
Buttprints. Lipprints.

They were laughing,
jumping in and out,

dancing at her wheelchair.
Her headscarf got wet.

When designs disappeared
the small one asked

Why does nothing last?
Evaporation, she said.

Never heard of it! he said.
She explained the way liquid

can change to air,
drawn to the sky

like rain in reverse,
going home.

BIOGRAPHICAL NOTE

Lisa C. Krueger is a clinical psychologist. Her poems have appeared in various journals, including *Plough-shares, Prairie Schooner, Nimrod,* and *Barrow Street.* She has published articles and written a series of in-teractive journals related to psychology and creativity. She maintains a psychotherapy practice in Pasadena focused on women's issues, health psychology, writing therapy, and the role of creativity in wellness.